A Collection of
POETRY
about Life

SHANNON ANDERSON

Fulton Books, Inc.
Meadville, PA

Published by Fulton Books 2021

ISBN 978-1-63860-831-8 (paperback)
ISBN 978-1-63860-832-5 (digital)

Printed in the United States of America

To my Lord and savior Jesus Christ for the gift of poetry. Then to my mom, Mrs. Essie P. Brown, and Aunt Argusta Taylor, who is deceased, for inspiring me to continue to write and never giving up on my dreams. I also would like to thank my friends Robert Caldwell and Earl Brooks for being my biggest cheerleaders and pushing me to make my dream become a reality in writing my first book.

Introduction

My name is Shannon Anderson, and I am fifty years of age. I began writing at the age of nineteen. I always loved to write, but after going to open mic night at Annie's art gallery, I really got more involved in poetry and wanted to pursue a career in it. I remember every time I would write a poem, I would call my mom, Mrs. Essie P. Brown, and my aunt Argusta Taylor and read my poems to them. When they weren't available, I would call my friends Robert Caldwell and Earl Brooks as I began to share my thoughts with them. No matter what the topic was, I was able to write a poem. I remember my first poem as if it was yesterday, "Single Momma Drama," because I was a single mom of two, one girl, named Jamesa McDonald, twenty-nine, and one son, William Anderson, twenty-five. When I read that poem at open mic night, everyone seemed to love it, and the audience cheered me on to continue to write. I thank God for the gift of poetry, and I want to encourage people in life that no matter what you go through, continue to be strong and persevere. I hope you enjoy reading my book as much as I have in writing it.

My Love

My love for you will never change
you're a part of me that I can't explain
when I'm around you I feel complete
my love for you will never grow weak

Our love is unique
and it grows stronger everyday
because as long as we stand
by each other we can
conquer anything that comes our way

My Story

It's time to come back home my child, you have lost your way
Inviting unsaved men into your life
Causing you, to go astray. I tried to warn you of these men
Time and time again.
It's time to wake up my child, aren't you tired of living in sin.
I gave you a peace of mind
I thought you'll be okay. I see you're still having problems
Trusting me to lead the way
I heard you crying in the night, it's going to be okay
I even handed you a tissue to wipe your tears away
I know you want to be married
I heard you time and time again
But you continue to be in bed with them even though you know
I hate sin. I am working on your behalf but the bitterness is still within
Learn how to forgive and finally let it go
Get into my word it will help you grow
Into the woman of God you desire to be
So when the time is right, you'll know your husband came from me.

I Will Never Get Married Again

I will never get married again
It's just something I don't want to do.
Spending my life loving a man
Who doesn't even appreciate you.
I gave you my love each and every day.
You never showed me you cared, now that love
Has faded away.
I will never get married again,
It's time for me to be free.
I'll just spend this time loving only me.

What Is a Father?

A father is a godly man, God created him from sand
He blew into his nostril the breath of life
He sent one to each household to watch over his children at night

He reads to me each night
While kissing me on my cheeks and saying good night
He's that person I tell all my dreams to
He even tries to make most of them come true
I watched him as he walked up and down the street
making sure each of his children had something to eat
he's always there to hand out advice
he's there for me and never thinks twice
you are my hero and I would like to say
I hope you have a Happy Father's Day

Encouragement

God will see you through he's coming to rescue you
He will never let you down
Because he's always somewhere around
When no one else will be there for you
Trust and believe he cares for you
Just stand on his word and keep the faith
He's always on time
He's never too late
So don't be discouraged no matter what you go through
The Lord will always be there to help you

Attitude Adjustments

People need attitude adjustments every day
Before you push all your loved ones away
Learn how to be patient that will really help you
And you will accomplish everything that you set out to do
Why are you so mad and walking around with a frown?
You should be thanking God you're still above ground
So, adjust your attitude and start today
You'll feel a lot better as you go from day to day

Cocaine

I'm a little bag just lying in the streets
Filled with white powdery substance
Why don't you try me
If you get a taste of my love
Honey I'll send you places you've never dreamed of
Shoot me in your veins
Let me take away your pain
You're feeling kind of down
Because no one wants you around
You've lost all hope now you're on dope
This high that you feel will never go away
You'll be begging for me
More and more each and every day
So don't try drugs it's not a game
All this powdery stuff will do is drive you insane.

Education

Education is the key to success
Encourage your children to do their best
Receive good grades reach for the star
Believe in yourself and you'll go far

Teachers work hard each and every day
To educate our children in every possible way
They teach us the skills that we need to know
and pray that we succeed no matter where we go

So get a good education and do your best
it will help you succeed and stand out from the rest

Friend

You're my friend and I can count on you
To say something funny when I'm mad
at you. You have my best interest at heart
and I see it every day.

It's in your eyes when I am hurting
wishing you could take the pain away.
You have given me strength to make it through
I'm so glad I found a true friend in you

Rain

As I sit down by my windowpane
I'm listening to the falling rain
wondering if the sun will come out again
and the rain will finally end

The grounds are wet the grass is green
this is what the rain will bring
the flowers are blooming every day
because the rain came down today

The birds are happy the kids can play
the forecast says no rain today

Now I like the rain it doesn't
hurt a thing
this is usually the first sign of spring

Is There Really a Man for Me?

Is there really a man for me?
If so then why is he hiding?
I'm home all alone sometimes
I sit right by my phone, waiting
For it to ring someday and the right man
Will be sent my way.

Waiting for me to love him
Comfort him and we could be friends
Sometimes I wish this lonely feeling will just end
It will my child just continue to pray
When the time is right
God will send him your way.

I Have to Find My Way Back Home

I have to find my way back home
Somehow I've lost my dreams.
In relationships after relationships, while my life went downstream.
I never took time out to see
what it was, that I really wanted to be.
I was hoping for a marriage, some children and maybe a career.
But all I got were lies from men, saying I love you dear.
Do they really know the true meaning of love.
It's not just a good time, a quick screw, and a back rub.
No I really missed out on all the things, that life could bring.
Wasting time after time, while my life went downstream.
Lord if you can give me a second chance, to capture my dreams
and hold off on romance.
Then maybe I can find the person, I used to be.
More better, more positive and finally free.
I have to find my way back home.

My Mother

The mother who came to be, she had one other child than me
her ways of overcoming her obstacles inspired me to believe
I can do all things through Christ that strengthens me
when things got rough you were always there
to hold my hand or comb my hair
you are my joy in the midst of the day
so enjoy yourself this Mother's Day

Have a Happy Mother's Day

Got Played

Girl you got played by the man of your dreams
everything he told you was not like it seems
he really hurt you by putting a hole in your heart
he took his marriage vows seriously
till death do us apart
you were the other woman
you knew it wouldn't last
time to pick up the pieces now
he's a part of your past

It's time to heal now it's going to be okay
you just have to take it slowly
as you endure every day
God will be with you every step of the way
remember he has your back
and he won't let you go astray
God has a man and he's designed just for you
and he will spend the rest of his life loving only you.

Alcohol

Alcohol is a drug it makes you weak
You can barely stand on your own two feet
Staggering everywhere and throwing up too
Having lots of headaches
And you don't know what to do
You don't remember the night before
Because your next-door neighbor
Had to carry you to your door
Now you're lying in bed and feeling blue
Your friends are all gone and your alcohol is too
Drinking alcohol will destroy you
You'll be experimenting so many
Hangovers you won't know what to do.

Anniversary

It's our anniversary we made it another year
We shared a lot of good times
We shared a lot of tears
We showed each other new ways to love
As we came home everyday
Our commitment got even stronger as we knelt down to
Pray

On your special day may you be reminded of the joy that's kept in
your heart
What God put together let no man tear apart

Depression

Depression is an illness
it will affect you
having you think about negative thoughts
by trying to control you
you will be having suicidal thoughts
running all through your head
saying little things like
you wish you were dead
depression is something
you don't have to go through
it's a mixture of emotions
that will destroy you
don't let depression
get a hold of you because
you'll lose interest in everything
that you once loved to do.

The Dream

Martin Luther King was a man who had a dream
He wanted everyone to be equal
no matter how hard it seemed
he walked the streets of Alabama day after day
joining people from all over as he helped lead the way

He had a voice that stood out
as he stood proud and tall
fighting for humanity and justice for all

He wasn't a violent man he didn't
put up a fight he just stood on
what he believed in and doing what was right

He wanted us not to be judged by the color of our skin
but accepted by the character that comes from within
as I look back over King's life he gave up a lot for you and me
He just wanted mankind to finally be free

King's vision he wanted to see overcome
was for blacks and whites standing together as one

I have a dream

Bus Driver

My bus driver is coming down the street,
Trying to be pleasant with everyone he meets.
Waiting for passengers that's his job,
But some people make it so very hard.

He lowers the lift so we can get on okay,
And he makes sure our smart trip is working properly
As we add on money from day to day.

He gets us to work on time and that's not all
When the bus is crowded
He drives very carefully, so we do not fall.
He's a citizen whom we care for a lot
He does his job so well and that's the best part
So when your bus driver does something nice for you,
Just take time out and say thank you.

He Loves Me

He means the world to me and this is true
I found myself in love with you
Falling in love once again
This time I hope it does not end
This thing called love is so unique
I found myself falling at your feet
Finding that person who makes all
Your dreams come true
When I look in your eyes that person is you

Justice

Where is justice in the world today?
People commit a crime and then walk away
why do we need a jury they sit on a stand
just being handpicked for cases
they don't quite understand

Coming to court every day trying to do their job
not paying attention to details
make decision-making so hard
having twelve jurors in the courtroom
trying to come to an agreement
as they walk away

(one week later)

The verdict is in, what does it say?
everyone found him guilty except for Mr. Day
being held back in the courtroom for hours of the day
we all have to agree or the murder can walk away
as Zimmerman stands before the judge
It's judgment day, the jurors don't have enough evidence
to lock that creep away

This poem is dedicated to Travon Martin
rest in peace my little brother

My Wedding Day

It's my wedding day
I can't wait to see
The man who God has chosen for me
As I walked down the aisle
To meet him that day.
I thank the Lord for sending him my way
Now he might not have everything that you
Want him too, but believe me my child
This one is right for you.

Deception

I met this man oh he was tight
Had a lot of moves and lines were just right
As he went on his way to capture my love
I said to myself this must be love
We exchanged numbers and parted that day
I thanked the Lord for sending him my way
As the relationship went on something was wrong
The phone rang all the time
He was never at home

I called one day, and someone picked up
It was the woman of the house what
I started to curse she asked me who would
You like to speak to as I began to explain
she said I'm his wife my head hung in shame
She must be lying I'm with him everyday
so I fell on my knees and began to pray

It was a couple weeks later that I saw the light
His father confirmed yes, she was his wife
I gave him a chance to try and explain
He said if I had told you I was married you wouldn't have given me
a chance
You took three years out of my life
You never told me that you had a wife
You were playing games right from the start
Taking advantage of my love and breaking my heart so women when
You think your man is true investigate him thoroughly it might be
other women and you.

My Love

The time has come for us
To say goodbye
While I walk away please don't cry
You are my love, you are my heart
The time has come for us to part
We'll meet each other
Once again you were
My lover and my friend

The Snow

The snow is the key to cleaning the earth
Falling from the sky in great big puffs
Some were heavy and some were light
Some of us even lost our lights
Some of us complained it interrupted our day
Shoveling the snow hoping it will melt away
Traffic jams when we tried to get something to eat
Grocery stores are crowded what no meats
Accidents everywhere there was nowhere to go
And all of this because of the snow
No trash pickups, no work, no school
No metro what sidewalks gone too
I'm getting cabin fever with nowhere to go
They cancel all activities because of the snow
We made snowmen and had lots of fun
Throwing snowballs too at everyone
We really wanted the snow to melt away
Because we got tired of shoveling our cars out
Day after day.

What Is a Mother?

A mother is someone you can look up to.
She's also someone I'll tell my dreams to.
When I'm hurting and can't sleep at night
She's that person that makes everything all right.

When I can't pray for myself, she's standing there
In the gap for me. Making sure the Lord will one day
Deliver me. She's my friend, my confidant, my strength
When I am weak. When I get knocked down from the things
Life throws my way, she encourages me to keep fighting
Because the Lord will make a way.

The Loss of a Loved One

Mourning the loss of a loved one seems so hard to do
but you have a circle of friends who care about you
You have to be strong, we will help you along.
Losing a family member always seems so wrong.
These things happen and we don't know what to say,
but if you need anything we're a phone call away.
We will be lifting you up in prayer today,
that God will ease your pain away.

Will I Ever See You Again?

Will I ever see you again by my side?
Where you can hide, I think about you wherever I go,
I just want you to know.
my love for you was so,
so true I miss being around you.
My love for you is here to stay,
I don't want it to go away.
It's deep inside and it's true
your hair, your eyes, I love everything about you.

I Don't Care

I just don't care anymore
and it's a shame, everywhere I go
people are all the same
using each other that's what they do best
just lovers of themselves
forgetting about the rest
This world is falling apart day by day
people are not about helping each other
they have truly gone astray
I just don't care anymore
you do what you wanna do
I'm not wasting any more time
worrying about the things that you do
I just don't care, leave me alone
I would rather be by myself,
than to have a bunch
of fake friends tagging along

The Gift

The gift that God has given to me was sending his son to set man free

He went about doing good from day to day. While praying to his
father to

Help lead the way. Jesus gave sight to the blind; he made the lame
to walk

He even made a dumb man talk. He went from city to city preaching
to everyone

So people could see God's love living through his only son people
annoyed him

and didn't even care they were the first ones to bring him to King
Pilate and

leave him there when Jesus went before King Pilate he asked what
did this man

Do everyone felt ashamed because their faces turned blue

They beat him and nailed him to the cross he went through

So much persecution so we wouldn't be lost.

In two days later the devil thought

He won. I finally got rid of God's only begotten son, but on the third day

He rose again conquering his victory so we could live again

So Christ's resurrection is reminding me of how God's love

Has set us free.

A Bitter Heart

I had a bitter heart and it showed every day.
I was so mad and confused, why? Because of being used.
I prayed to God every day that he will take the hurt away.
I meditated on his word night after night while crying in my spirit
"God please make it all right" 'God answered my prayers and
Now I am new all glory and honor belongs to you.

Having an open mind to love again being washed away from
The bitterness within. You can't let hatred consume
In your heart, all it will do is tear you apart.
You have to divorce the bitterness from within
Because nothing good will be able to come in.

Deadbeat Dads

Deadbeat dads are growing rapidly every day
Just making babies and then walking away
leaving them with their grandparents
To care for them all alone
Not offering any type of support and we know that this is wrong
How can you bring a child into this world?
And do the things that you do you think everybody should
Be taking care of that child except you

You're a deadbeat dad and that's a shame
You should be posted on Facebook
So everybody would know your name
So if you are out here making babies
And you know that's you
Stop thinking everybody else should
Be raising your child except you.

Don't Give Up

Don't give up and you sometimes will
It feels like your life is going downhill.
You ask why am I here? Do you really want to know
Sometimes you have to go with the flow
Don't give up it's not in God's will
He will direct you, you just be still

(The test)
We all go through life facing some kind of test
Wondering if God will give us some rest
Not always knowing, what the master has planned
Trying to trust him, even when we don't understand
Our purposes in life and what we must go through
Knowing in our hearts
He will see us through
This thing called life as he prepares the way
By showing his children how to be strong and pray
I've had some disappointments, setbacks, and detours along
The way but I stayed in my word so I would not go astray
Time is near and I know this to be true.
Don't ever give up on God because he won't give up on you.

Hold On

Hold on and don't let go you're closer to your breakthrough than you'll ever know. So when you see others being blessed just remind yourself it's only a test. God wants to see what you will do when it seems like he has forgotten about you. Faith and endurance works hand in hand God already knows what he has planned. So trust and believe he cares for you. It won't be long before he blesses you. So continue to do your very best and let God handle all the rest.

Time to Heal

It's time to fall in love with myself again
Stop lowering your standard to be with these men
Take the time to really see if they have good intentions w
Having a healthy relationship without all of the fussin
And putting me down with your constant criticizing
When I'm not around
You say I'm conflicting that may be true
I see myself falling out of love with you
I'm a good woman why can't you see
If you can't build me up, then set me free
Another good man will come my way
And he will make sure I'm loved each and every day
Oh, I can't wait to finally see
The man who God created just for me.
It's time to heal

Better Days

write because I'm feeling, I'm feeling so much pain
ot having anyone to talk to it's driving me insane
rying to pray to God each and every day
o lighten all of my burdens and wipe my tears away
My heart is so broken I'm crying out to thee
ord when are you coming to finally rescue me
m tired of living in a world that is so cold
ut I am trying my best to stand on your word
nd do what I was told
s not easy Lord feeling all alone
ut knowing I can rely on your strength
know I can go on
etter days are coming I just have to wait and see
ou promised if I accept your son
ou're coming back for me
My better days are coming.

God Is Real

God is real, how do you know?
He protects me and provides for me wherever I go
When I'm up at night dealing with life
I hear a small still voice
Saying my child it will be all right
So as you go through life and you're faced with a test just come into
my arms and I will give you rest learn how to trust me
He asked why is that so hard for you to do
Don't you know by now
Who is keeping you
Trials and tribulations they will come your way
But now is not the time for you to go astray.

Christ Lives

Christ lives, Christ lives
He lives in the world today
He walks with me and he talks with me
Along life's narrow way
If you want to find the true light today
Give God your heart and begin to pray
Ask for forgiveness for all your sins
Today is the day your new life begins.

Homeless

I'm homeless, I have nowhere to stay
Everywhere I've looked for work
People are turning me away
I'm on these streets begging for money every day
Because these hunger pains
Inside just won't go away
Don't look at me, as if I am a bum on these streets
I fell on hard times because of losing my jobs
Now it's so hard to get back on my feet
Because everywhere I looked for work
People think I am a bum on these streets
Don't judge me, I went to school and earned my degree but now the job market is so tight they won't even hire me.

Lord Show Me the Way

Lord show me the way
Read the Bible and learn how to pray
We need your direction and guidance every day
The world is in a turmoil
Lord show us the way
Jesus Christ died and gave the perfect plan
He said my child take hold of my hand
My father in heaven he loves you so much
He created us in his own image with one special touch. Salvation is here and he awaits today
If you want to be saved cry out Lord show me the way.

The Promise

God please renew my mind every day
Watch over me too while I pray
I need your presence as we speak
My flesh is tired and I'm growing weak
Trying to study your word day after day
So I don't fall into temptation and then go astray
The devil is busy leading people straight to hell
Because he is clever in the lies he tells
He leads you into a life of sin
Because he knows his time is near the end
So be very careful while we wait and pray
Because the Lord is coming back one day
He's going to crack these skies you just have to wait and see. He promised he's coming back for you and me. Oh I can't wait to finally be with all my family who died before me.

The Nosey co-worker

The nosey co-worker we all have them on the job
Spreading rumors every day like it's their second job

Coming to work gathering information from day to day
Just running their mouth is what they do all day

When will they ever mind their own business?
And leave yours alone, I forgot you don't have any because you're all alone
Mind your own business why is that so hard to do
Oh, I forgot nobody on the job likes being around you
You're the complainer, the troublemaker and busybody
Walking around here every day

You always say you don't need this job so
Why are you here every day?

Dealing with My Issues

Lord help me with my issues
That I encounter every day
I need some type of outlet
To help me along the way
Help me while I pray to you
By keeping my mind stayed on you
Trying to be positive and I have to be strong
I'm suffocating with my issues making me question where I went wrong
As I look back over my life
I'm trying my best to see
Why can't I be normal
Why can't my mind be free
Sending me on pity parties
And bad memories of my past
It's suffocating me so much
Please bring this guilt to pass
I have so many questions
That I need answers to
I'm trying to be patient Lord
As I continue to wait on you.
I'm dealing with my issues.

Lost

Satan is trying his best to destroy my mind
Having me thinking serving you is a waste of my time
You said if I keep my mind stayed on you
You'll guide my steps and see me through
I don't feel your presence Lord have I lost my way?
You used to talk to me each and every day
Have my sins gotten in the way Lord
From me hearing from you
I need your help now
Don't know what to do I'm trying to live my life
The best way I can going through so much prosecution that I don't
quite understand I'm tired Lord and I'm losing my faith just don't
know how much more of this life I can take.
I'm lost.

Downsize Economy

Trying to survive in this economy is hard
low-paying wages people competing for jobs
trying to figure out which bills to pay
kids need clothes put them on layaway
everything is getting higher people are getting stressed
worrying at night when you should be getting rest some of us turn to
the bottle looking for hope
some of us even tried using some dope
shopping spending money that you don't even have driving in the
streets and you're about to crash
You blame everyone for your life
taking a fall
Feeling, hopeless, restless and very small get out there and change
your life
sometimes you just have to sacrifice
you have the talent to bring you some cash
so stop all the whining and get off your ass.

Coronavirus Poem

I am a virus that started in Wuhan, China you see
In a couple of weeks, the CDC couldn't contain me.
Coming to the United States was my final destination
Interrupting your lives and causing devastation
I took away your jobs and crashed your economy too
Everyone blamed the president because of what he knew
I closed your churches, your schools, casinos and so much more
Now that I have your attention, come sit down I will tell you more
I have you wearing masks because I'm a different type of disease
And I spread very quickly with a cough or a sneeze
I linger in the air for a minute or two, leaving my droplets behind if only you knew
The doctors say washing your hands for 20 seconds will make me go away
But the information they have changes from day to day
I have new cases being reported and I'm rising every week
Leaving them confused when this thing will really peak
I attack the young, the old, ones with underlying conditions too
It's no telling how much damage I will do.
My victim's lungs are very weak, fighting for their lives as we do speak
You ask why is this happening, what have we done
The nation has turned their backs on God's only son
Now the wrath of God is here to stay, and only God alone can take this virus away.
My name is COVID-19.

Broken Spirits

Broken spirit crushed in my own image
Drained in pain, mind going insane
Everyone I tried to reach out to didn't even care
I was drowning alone in my own despair
Looking for a way out of this mess
Trying my best to pass every test
So many questions Lord I had for you
Not quite understanding
What you were taking me through
Trying to cover it up was part of my game
Not realizing it was bringing shame to your name
I use to be a child of the almighty king standing on your word not accepting everything trying to fit into a world that was so cold
Not obeying your word, not doing what I was told
Then one day I lost my way the devil came in he wanted to play. He got into my head time and time again then I saw myself slipping back into a life full of sin. A couple years later. I woke up it was just a disguise. I had let Satan come in my life and with him I abide. As I began to pray Holy Spirit help lead the way. Safety back into my father's arms again. With him I have conquered some peace from within these broken spirits.

My Trip to Heaven

If I can go to heaven, I promise not to cry
Just want to see my aunt again
So I can tell her hi
Heaven was rejoicing when she gained her wings that day God knew
you were tired of suffering
So he came and took you away
The Lord is too wise he doesn't make a mistake
Your death was very sudden to me
My heart just had to break
But then the Lord reminded me
She will be with you every day
As long as you accept my son
You'll see her again one day
Then all of my children will finally be free
You have to be strong and hang in there with me.

Wake Up

Lord we need a touch from you
Without your presence what shall we do
In a world that is so lost and confused
Tired of being hurt, abandoned and abused
Life has its ups and downs this much is true
But I'm trying to hang in there by trusting you
Even when I can't see my way. I'm following your footsteps as you lead the way
The world needs to heal now they don't know what to do because they don't understand why we can't make it without you.
The Lord has delivered us time and time again, but we continue to disobey him by living in our sin time to wake up y'all the Lord is speaking loud and
Clear. He can crack these skies any day now and if you are not ready, he will leave you here.

Faith

Have faith if you believe in God
even when your life seems hard
don't give up he'll be there for you
and give you strength to make it through
patience and endurance works hand in hand
God already knows what he has planned
so trust and believe he will protect you
and keep the devil from harming you
so continue to do your very best
and let God handle all the rest.

Get Well

As I'm sitting in the hospital room looking at you
I'm waiting for the day when God heals you
it hurts so bad that you're suffering this way
I'm kneeling by your bedside as I began to pray
asking God to give me strength to make it through
my heart is heavy now I can't find my way
it's getting harder and harder to face another day
as I began to close my prayer to you
Lord please heal their body and make them new
the doctor gave up and walked away
I trust you have the final say

Lord Help Me

Lord if you could help me out of this mess
so my life will soon be blessed
free from sin and free from all
help me o Lord when I call
the devil is busy, please stay away
you have the weapon learn how to pray
so when you feel all alone
don't pick up somebody's phone
talk to me you know what to do
I have given you the strength to make it through
this world that seem so confused
my child, my child you cannot lose
so walk in victory and start today remember this learn how to pray.

Forgotten

God I was broken couldn't see my way through
I've even felt like giving up on life
because I fail short in trusting you, seeing others being blessed
who didn't acknowledge you
so I began to doubt what my savior could really do
you took me on a journey and showed me how you blessed me in the
past and so much more
I see you have forgotten about all of the open doors
I was there when your friends walked out on you
helping you to be strong because I believed in you
I was there protecting you each and every night
providing your every need making sure you continue to fight
even when you felt alone and you didn't know what to do
I reached down with my loving arms and began to carry you
I don't know what I have to do to make you understand
just continue to believe in me and trust the master's plan.

Unforgiveness

Unforgiveness is something I struggle with from day to day
the hatred that I'm feeling inside just won't go away
I try and be happy I'm trying to be strong
but the burdens of my past just won't leave me alone

Trying to be to myself want people to leave me alone
I feel like I'm down here on this earth
not really knowing where I belong
wanting to be free from the ghost of my past

This feeling of guilt just cannot last
I will continue to wait on you
I need your help don't know what to do
as I lay down and go to sleep today
I hope you help me find my way with forgiveness

Computers

Computers are taking over can't you see
we're losing our jobs constantly
they are doing everything that we used to do
from searching for jobs, answering phones and paying our bills too
we depend on them so much that it's a shame by logging on to them
up pops our names we think we are moving forward from day to day
but technology is destroying us in so many ways
we're getting lazy as a generation each and every day
we forgot how to think because computers got in the way
computers are taking jobs from you and me
I don't understand why everyone can't see
this is the new millennium that has come our way
computers are taking over and walk-in interviews are fading away
everything is online as we speak if you don't have a computer
you won't be able to compete
in this new job market today
having computer skills is needed or the employer will turn you away.

Doubt

Doubt is a word I'm not used to
I still want to believe my dreams can come true
It's hard for me to see my way
The devil is busy every day
I try and keep my focus on you but
sometimes I fail in trusting you
I know that all things are working out
For my good like you say
I just hope to see a brighter day
A brighter day is near I just have to wait and see
Because God is coming to finally rescue me.
When I increase my faith and remove the doubt
He's going to bring me out
Of all my worries and my fears
He's going to dry up all my tears
So I have to be strong and continue to wait
The Lord is always on time he's never too late
So increase your faith and remove the doubt
God is going to bring me out
To the other side just wait and see
He's always concerned about you and me

Homeless

I saw a man standing on the streets
He was begging everyone for money
So he could get something to eat
Walking over to this young man
I wanted to meet
His feet were bleeding bad
From the glass that was in his feet
He said young lady can you buy me some shoes
The ones that I am wearing are badly used
Reaching in my pocket.
I handed him some change
He smiled at me as he mentioned his name
The conversation that we had was totally sane
This man was homeless
So when you see a man standing in the streets
Don't be so quick to judge him take time out to speak

Covid 19 Vaccines

There are three vaccines out here you see
Trying their best to get rid of me
taking one and two shots hoping this virus go away
But are they really the answers the world need's today?

Where did these vaccines come from?
Can anybody see this is the new method in trying to kill me
Did we fast, pray and trust in God to take this virus away.
We tried our way it's been a year
But COVID 19 is not disappearing
And we are living in fear
Getting vaccinated was their plan but we
are still trusting in the wrong man
No one has the cure to make this go away
Because we are still not listening to what God is trying to say
Through this virus that is killing everyone
God is mad at the world and his wrath is not done.
The world needs to repent and turn from their evil ways
Then Jesus can intercede and ask God to take COVID away.

Single Momma Drama

I'm a single momma and I'm all alone.
Everytime I turn around a man is on my phone
telling me he loves me and all this stuff
The lies and deceit I had enough
You say you love me and I believe that's true but everytime I see you
You say we're through.
I thought you were the black knight taking me away
But instead you were the devil in disguise.
Easing all of my dreams away
Who is this man who stands before me.
Making promises of marriage and that's the way it's gonna be
Somebody smack me back into reality
I was blind but now I see you really weren't the man for me.

What is a Mother?

A mother is a good listener always giving out advice
In helping her children the best way she can
Through hard work and sacrifice

Everyone can not be a mother
It's a gift from above
She has to have a genuine heart
That's filled with so much love

A mother's love for her children
Is teaching them right from wrong
And when her children feel like giving up
She helps them right along

In setting goals for her children
She builds their self -esteem
And no matter what happens in life
She still encourages them to dream

The Unemployed

I'm unemployed! I don't know what to do.
I've been looking for work
But nothing is coming through
Applied online, that's even a joke
Did my resume go through?

What! The computer is broke!!!
Lying in bed can't seem to get ahead
Bills piling up kids need to be fed
Trying to land a job, seem so hard to do
But I can't give up now... I must keep pushing my way through!

As I sit back and watch people go to work every day
It's getting harder and harder to face another day
I must keep believing God will make a way
But my mind keeps doubting and fear gets in the way
God has something in store for you...
So, stop all the complaining and praise your way through!

Love doesn't live here anymore·

Love is Just an illusion
Inside my head
People would say anything
To get you in bed

They lie and cheat it's part of their game
But when we turn the tables on them
It's you they want to blame

They all say baby I will never cheat
It's a different story when you're lying in bed
Underneath those sheets

Are there any honest people out here anymore?
Who haven't been hurt or abused
I know I'm a good person just tired of being used

Maybe love does exist and maybe it will come my way
But even if it doesn't I'll still be ok.

About the Author

Shannon Anderson is fifty years of age. After attending open mic night at Annie's art gallery, Shannon got more involved into poetry. She remembers every time she would write a poem, she would call her aunt and her mom just to share her thoughts with them. She remembers her first poem as if it was yesterday, "Single Momma Drama," because she is a single mom of two. After she read that poem at open mic night, everyone seemed to love it and encouraged her to continue to write. She thanks God for this gift of poetry, and she wants to encourage people in life that no matter what you go through, continue to be strong and persevere. She hopes you enjoy reading her book as much as she has in writing it.

CPSIA information can be obtained
at www.ICGtesting.com
Printed in the USA
BVHW082154220122
626944BV00005B/215

9 781638 608318